Nico & Lola

Kindness Shared Between a Boy and a Dog

by Meggan Hill 🐾 photography by Susan M. Graunke

HARPER

An Imprint of HarperCollinsPublishers

Acknowledgments

Special thanks to: Kathy Allegretti • Sarah Barthel • Sandra Bialek • Jacki Caskey • Norah Caskey • Melinda Copp • Laura Crawford • Marie Cummings • Joseph Curran • Greg Dunn • Jane Fitzgerald • Jerry Graunke • Madeline Graunke • Terence Graunke • Barbara Hagenson • Dawn Havrelock • Linda Hawver • Jamee Riggio Heelan • Esther Hershenhorn • Francie Hill • Mia Hill • Rose Jallits • Marion Johnson • Max Kanter • Pam Kaster • Hazel Kloempken • Kristen Knecht • JoAnn Kowalski • Shawn Lamb • Marc Landsberg • Lori Magee • Kate Pattee-Malak • Karen McDiarmid • Stacie McManus • Diane McQueeney • Lisa McQueeney • Vincent McQueeney • Gita Mekyte • Jill Mills • Kourtney Mulcahy • Claire Novak • Yvonne Ocrant • Debbie Olinger • Andy Pataky • Lisa Peelo • Jenny Powell • Nancy Reimers • Esmeralda Rodriguez • Evangelina Rodriguez • Javier Rodriguez • Natalie Rompella • Elayne Schulman • Beth Snodgrass • Anthony Tortoriello • Betsy Watz • Kay Younggreen

To my kind family—
those with two legs and those with four
—M.H.

To Terry, Jerry, and Maddie
for their unconditional support and enthusiasm,
and to my precious mom, who taught me that reading
opens up new and exciting worlds for each of us
—S.M.G.

It was a regular kind of day when suddenly the phone rang.

Nico's momma said, "This telephone call is for you."

Nico listened to his aunt Sue on the phone.

"I need to go away for the weekend. I know my dog, Lola, will miss me. Would you be *so kind* as to take care of my little girl?"

Nico quickly answered, "Sure, Aunt Sue. I *think* I can do it!"

All of Nico smiled.

Nico and his momma went inside for lemonade.

Nico wondered, How will I be *so kind*?

Still, he could not wait for tomorrow, when Lola would arrive.

Nico would think of ways to be so kind.

After breakfast, Nico heard his momma call, "They're here!"

Nico rushed outside and stretched out his arm to welcome Lola.

He wanted to give the small pug a chance to get to know him.

"Good morning, Lola!" he said.

Nico grinned as Lola sniffed the back of his hand with her wet little nose.

Being kind is smiling at someone new.

Nico and Lola ran straight for the backyard to play tag.

"You're it!" he told her.

After a few games, Lola began huffing and puffing.

Nico looked into Lola's dark chocolate eyes.

He asked, "What's wrong? Are you thirsty, Girl?"

Nico brought Lola a bowl of cool water.

Being kind is showing concern for others.

The following day, Nico's neighbors came over to play with Lola.

They sat in the thick green grass and brushed Lola's smooth black coat.

Nico tickled Lola's pudgy tummy.

Lola turned her head and nudged Nico's knuckles for more.

When it was time for a walk, Nico showed the girls how to gently hold Lola's leash.

The friends had fun all afternoon.

Being kind is setting a good example.

Early the next morning, Nico took Lola outside.

He pulled a small dog bone from the front pocket of his jeans.

He held it behind his back and said, "I have a special snack for you!"

Lola politely nibbled the treat.

"Thank you," she seemed to say, licking the crumbs from Nico's fingers, wagging her tail, and wiggling her whole body.

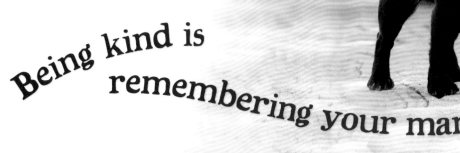

Being kind is remembering your manners.

Then Lola crawled into Nico's lap.

"YOU are *so-oooooo* cute," he sweetly told her.
"I love your curly-whirly tail."

Nico talked on and on to Lola, telling her all
about school and Momma's cupcakes and even
butterflies.

Lola tilted her head and perked her ears, paying
close attention.

Being kind is being a good listener.

Later they found Nico's dad cleaning the garage.

Nico asked, "Can Lola and I help?"

Dad answered, "You bet! I can always use an extra set of hands and paws."

Nico picked up the big green broom and got to work sweeping out the dust.

Lola wanted to play, but instead she waited patiently.

She stayed right beside Nico's sneakers the whole time.

Being kind is sticking together until the job is done.

Afterward Nico said, "Let's go play in the dirt, Squirt!"

The two friends walked down the path together while Dad followed.

First Nico led Lola.

Then Lola led Nico.

Sometimes they stayed side by side.

When Lola wanted to stop and sniff the dirt, Nico waited for her.

And when Nico wanted to stop and study the anthill, Lola waited for him.

Being kind is taking turns.

As they reached the house, Lola began to limp.

Her face wrinkled with worry when she held up her sore leg.

"Oh no, Lola. I think you need help!" Nico said.

Lola sat very still while Nico removed a small pebble stuck between her toes.

He asked, "Want me to kiss it and make it all better?"

Lola snorted and danced in circles on her mended paw.

Nico giggled.

Being kind is helping others in need.

That evening, Lola plopped herself down on Nico's favorite blanket.

Then she yawned.

Nico curled up next to her and whispered, "You're snug as a pug on a rug."

Lola fell fast asleep.

Nico grinned while Lola began to snore, "Zzz—zzz—zzzzzzz . . ."

Being kind is sharing even your favorite blanket.

LOLA

Lola's last morning arrived much too soon.

When Aunt Sue came to pick her up, Nico did not want Lola to go.

But when Lola saw Aunt Sue, the little pug squealed with delight.

Nico knew. "You're happy, Girl, aren't you?"

As hard as it was, Nico gave Lola's leash back to Aunt Sue.

Being kind is giving from the heart.

Nico sat down beside Lola and looked into her round face.

"I'm going to miss you, Lola."

Lola let out a soft "*Woof*" and placed her front paws on his knees.

"I know, Girl," Nico said.

His hand rested on the back of her velvety neck.

"You'll miss me too."

Then Nico bent over and hugged Lola tightly.

Being kind is treating others the way you want to be treated.

Nico took a deep breath and asked, "Aunt Sue, will you take good care of *our* girl?"

Aunt Sue knelt close to him.

"I always will," she promised.

Nico beamed and wrapped both arms around her.

Aunt Sue asked, "Nico, may I tell my other friends how you were *so kind* to Lola? Maybe you can help them out too?"

Nico quickly answered, "Sure, Aunt Sue. I *know* I can do it."

Once again, all of Nico smiled.

Being kind is making our world a better place.

Pass it on!